AF456795

A Monster Traffic Jam

Written by Kay Woodward
Illustrated by Richard Watson

It was another fine day on Make It Street.

'What shall we do today?' asked Scooter.

'I know!' exclaimed Cora. 'Let's visit the city farm.'

Soon, the bus arrived, and Ralf, Scooter, Netty, and Cora got on. They paid the driver and found four empty seats.

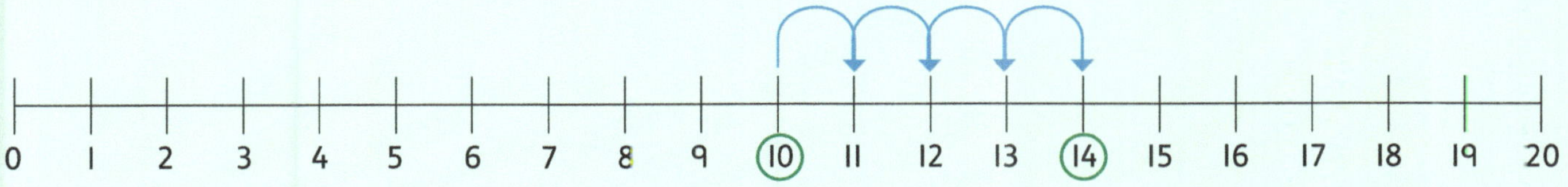

0 1 2 3 4 5 6 7 8 9 10 11 12 13 14 15 16 17 18 19 20

There were ten monsters on the bus. **Then** Ralf, Scooter, Netty, and Cora got on the bus, so there were four more monsters. **How many** monsters are on the bus **now**? Use the number line to help you.

The bus trundled through the city. It went past the school and the park.

'Is it lunchtime yet?' asked Scooter. 'I've brought sandwiches!'

'Let's eat them when we get to the farm,' suggested Ralf.

Then, with a squeak of brakes, the bus stopped.

'It's just a traffic jam,' called the bus driver. 'I'm sure we won't be stuck here for long.'

However, the bus didn't move. The traffic jam just got longer.

'The city farm will be closed by the time we get there!' cried Netty.

First, there were three cars in the queue behind the bus. **Then** five more cars joined the queue. **How many** cars are in the queue **now**?

Just **then**, a goat trotted past the bus.

'That's odd,' said Ralf.

Next, Scooter spotted a cow.

Look! A cow!

Then, Cora spotted some ducks.

Ducks!

0 1 2 3 4 5 6 7 8 9 10 11 12 13 14 15 16 17 18 19 20

First, Cora saw two ducks. **Then** she saw four more. **How many** ducks did she see **in total**? Use the number line to work out the **addition**.

The monsters got off the bus to find out what was happening.

There were farm animals running everywhere. The animals were the cause of the traffic jam!

'We were going to the farm,' Cora said, 'but the farm has come to us!'

Moo!
Baa!
Quack!

Just **then**, a farmer hurried over, looking worried. 'All of the animals have escaped from the city farm!' he said.

'Don't worry,' said Scooter, smiling. 'We will help you to get them back.'

‘Let’s round up the animals!’ said Netty. ‘I will round up the cows.’

She began to walk slowly towards four cows.

'I'll get the ducks!' said Cora.

She found the ducks and carefully lifted up four of them. Two more waddled after her.

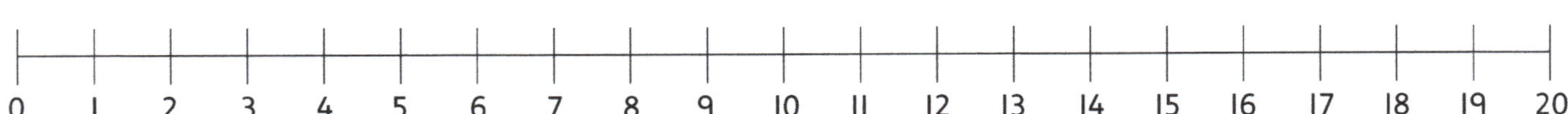

Netty rounded up four cows. Cora rounded up six ducks. **How many** animals did they round up **altogether**? Use the number line to help you.

'I will round up the sheep,' said Ralf. He rounded up eight sheep **altogether**.

Baa!

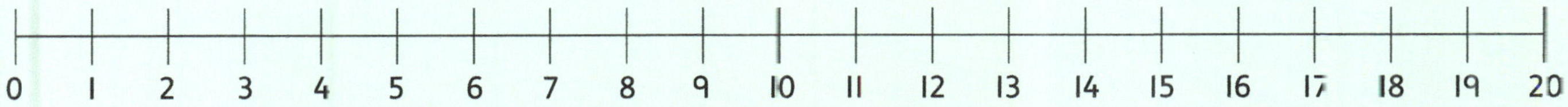

0 1 2 3 4 5 6 7 8 9 10 11 12 13 14 15 16 17 18 19 20

Together, Netty and Cora rounded up ten animals. Ralf rounded up eight more. **Count on** to work out 10 + 8. Use the number line to help you.

Meanwhile, Scooter looked for the goat. He couldn't find it anywhere!

He looked by the bus stop.

He looked in the shops.

He looked under a bench ... but he couldn't find the goat.

Then Scooter looked through the bus window. The goat was on the bus!

'I've found the goat!' cried Scooter. 'And the goat has found my sandwiches!'

Ralf, Netty, and Cora rounded up eighteen animals. **Now** Scooter has found the goat! **Count on** to work out 18 + 1.

Now Scooter knew how to get the goat to follow him.

He got on the bus and grabbed the rest of his sandwiches. **Then** he climbed off the bus again ... and the goat trotted after him!

First, the goat found one sandwich. **Then** it found five more. **How many** sandwiches did the goat find **altogether**?

‘Let’s go!’ called Scooter, marching towards the city farm.

He was followed by one goat, four cows, six ducks, eight sheep … and three monsters!

When they got to the city farm, Scooter led the animals in through the front gate.

Ralf spotted a gap in the fence. ‘That must be where the animals got out,’ he said. ‘We can fix it.’

The farmer handed out some tools. The monsters got to work fixing the fence and helping him with some other jobs.

They built a scratching post for the cows.

They dug a pond for the ducks.

They built a wool washer for the sheep.

They built a playhouse for the goat.

The animals showed how happy they were by making lots of noise.

Outside the city farm, a queue of visitors began to grow.

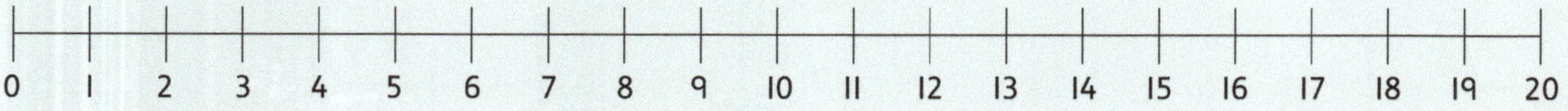

0 1 2 3 4 5 6 7 8 9 10 11 12 13 14 15 16 17 18 19 20

First, there were two people in the queue at the gate. **Then** thirteen more people joined the queue. **How many** people were in the queue **altogether**? Use the number line to help you.

‘**Now**, the city farm is monstrously good!’ said the farmer. ‘To say thank you, here are some free passes to come back any time.’

The monsters whooped!

Help keep the animals in!

The farmer has put a lock on the city farm gate. Help him to unlock the gate by working out the **additions**. Use the number line to help you.